BOOK 4

FOUR STAR

SIGHT READING AND EAR TESTS

DAILY EXERCISES FOR PIANO STUDENTS

BY BORIS BERLIN AND ANDREW MARKOW

Series Editor

SCOTT McBRIDE SMITH

National Library of Canada Cataloguing in Publication Data

Berlin, Boris, 1907-2001
    Four star sight reading and ear tests [music]

ISBN 0-88797-789-8 (Introductory level). —
ISBN 0-88797-791-X (bk. 1). — ISBN 0-88797-793-6 (bk. 2)
ISBN 0-88797-795-2 (bk. 3). — ISBN 0-88797-797-9 (bk. 4)
ISBN 0-88797-799-5 (bk. 5). — ISBN 0-88797-801-0 (bk. 6)
ISBN 0-88797-803-7 (bk. 7). — ISBN 0-88797-805-3 (bk. 8)
ISBN 0-88797-807-X (bk. 9). — ISBN 0-88797-809-6 (bk. 10)

1. Piano — Studies and exercises. 2. Ear training.
3. Sight-reading (Music) I. Markow, Andrew, 1942- II. Title.

MT236.B473 2002   786.2'142'076   C2002-900877-8

FREDERICK
HARRIS
MUSIC

© Copyright 2002 The Frederick Harris Music Co., Limited
All Rights Reserved

ISBN 0-88797-797-9

PREFACE

The ability to read music at sight at the piano is an important skill for all musicians. As piano students work toward fluency in sight reading, develop aural proficiency, and gain a practical knowledge of theory, they will build a foundation of musicianship that will help them to understand music throughout their lives.

Are some pianists naturally better sight readers than others? Not really. But some recognize patterns on the printed page more readily. Such students use their **visual learning skills**. Other students use their natural **tactile sense** to move around the keyboard quickly. Still others have an innate **aural ability** to hear both melody and harmony with only a glance at the score. Some students may also apply **analytical skills** learned from a study of theory to understand form and content.

The goal of the *Four Star* series is to develop each of these skills and abilities in equal measure. In the process of completing the *Four Star* series, students will improve not only their sight-reading skills but also their proficiency in learning and memorizing music. They will also expand their coordination of eyes, ears, and hands, and their powers of concentration and observation. As a result, *Four Star* students will develop confidence in themselves and in their musical abilities and performance.

Each of the 11 *Four Star* volumes contains daily exercises in sight reading and ear training and builds a foundation for an analytical approach to sight reading music, using examples taken from the standard repertoire. (Some excerpts have been modified by the authors for pedagogical reasons.)

Completion of each *Four Star* book effectively prepares students for the corresponding level of examination systems, including:

- RCM Examinations
- Certificate of Merit (Music Teachers Association of California)
- National Guild of Piano Teachers
- most MTNA curriculums

In order to develop students' reading and overall musical abilities more fully, the authors have chosen to exceed the requirements of most examination systems.

How to Use This Book

The purpose of the *Four Star* series is to provide daily exercises in sight reading and ear training for students to practice at home, as well as tests to be given by the teacher at the lesson. Best results will be obtained through daily student practice, and consistent monitoring and testing at the lesson by the teacher.

SIGHT READING AND RHYTHM

The daily sight-reading and rhythm exercises are intended for students to do by themselves. There are five exercises per week, each including a short piece and clapping rhythm. A reference section on Musical Elements and Patterns in This Volume can be found on pp. 4–6. It is useful for teachers to review these at the lesson.

EAR TRAINING

Ear-training exercises can be found following the sight-reading and rhythm drills. These, too, are designed to be practiced by the student alone, as assigned by the teacher.

TESTS

Tests are found beginning on p. 37. These are designed to be given by the teacher at the lesson at the conclusion of the corresponding week's work. Supplementary material may be found in the series *Melody Playback/Singback* and *Rhythm Clapback/Singback* by Boris Berlin and Andrew Markow.

SUPPLEMENTAL MATERIAL

Twenty-seven additional pieces can be found beginning on p. 49. These will give students additional preparation before they begin work on Level 5. Students should play these with their teacher at the lesson, or as assigned for home practice.

Musical Elements and Patterns in This Volume

DIRECTIONS OF A MELODY

Notes move up.

Notes move down.

Five notes move up, then change direction.

Four notes move down, then change direction.

Several changes of direction
(a zig-zag movement).

Repeated notes (the notes remain the same).

A turn (see p. 39).

MELODY AND ACCOMPANIMENT

Melody (see p. 7)

Accompaniment

Melody (see p. 51)

Accompaniment

Sequence (see p. 18)

Melodic Repetition (see p. 25)

INTERVALS

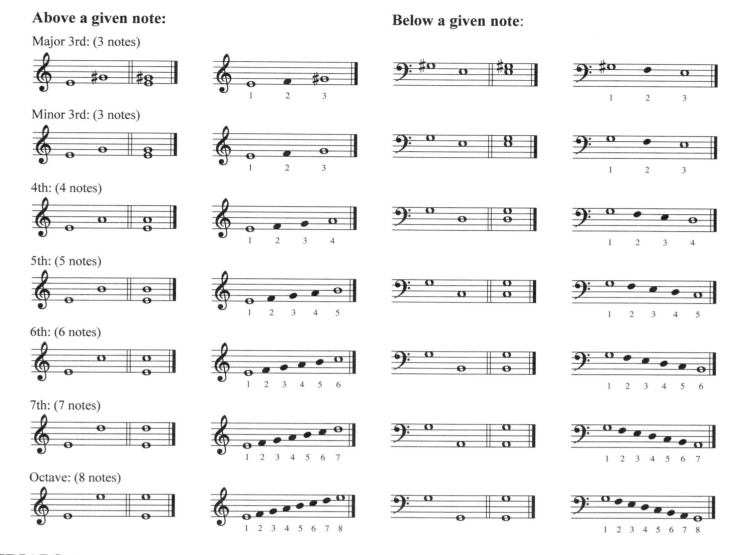

TRIADS (Three-note Chords)

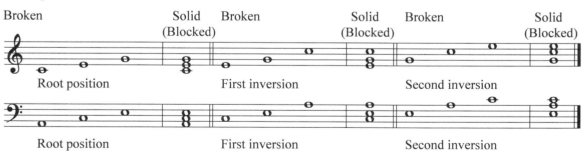

EXAMPLES OF INTERVALS AND TRIADS FOUND IN PIECES

A major triad (chord tones)   (see p. 13)

4th m 3rd 6th

m 3rd   (see p. 14)

TIME VALUES

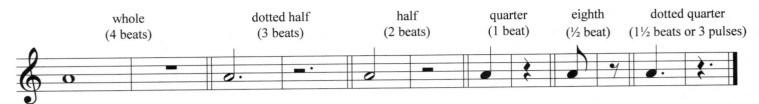

RHYTHMIC PATTERNS

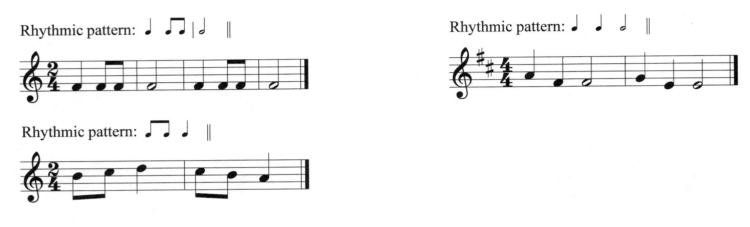

RHYTHMIC IMITATION

(see p. 11)

(see p. 12)

MARKS OF EXPRESSION AND OTHER MUSICAL SIGNS

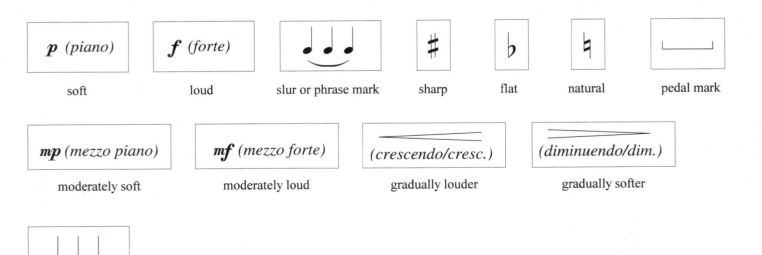

DAILY SIGHT-READING EXERCISES No. 1

Directions to the student: Complete one set of sight-reading exercises at each practice session.

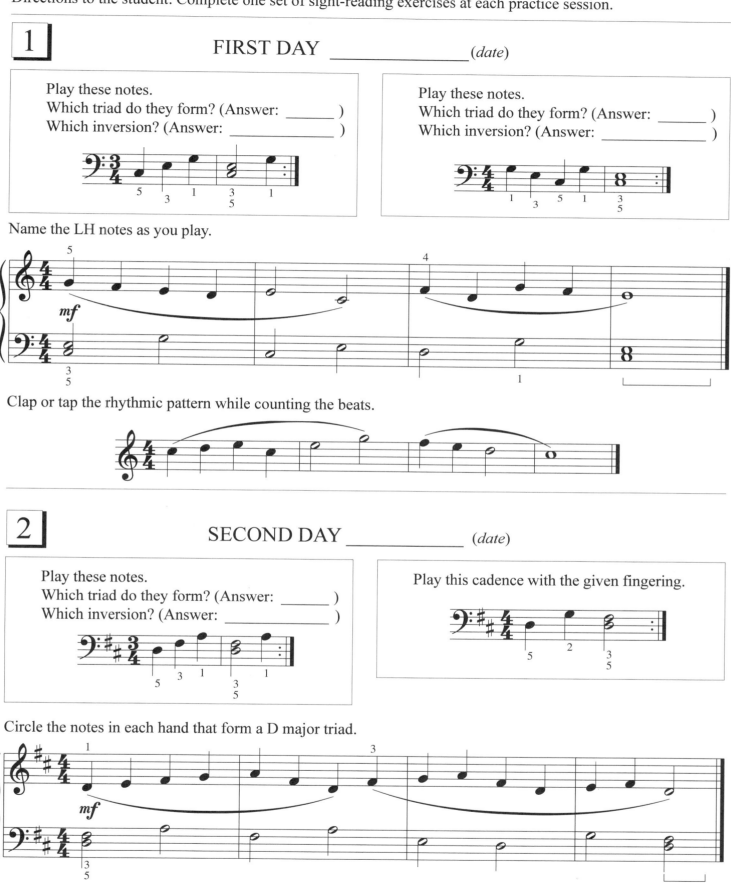

1 FIRST DAY _____ (*date*)

Play these notes.
Which triad do they form? (Answer: _____)
Which inversion? (Answer: _____)

Play these notes.
Which triad do they form? (Answer: _____)
Which inversion? (Answer: _____)

Name the LH notes as you play.

Clap or tap the rhythmic pattern while counting the beats.

2 SECOND DAY _____ (*date*)

Play these notes.
Which triad do they form? (Answer: _____)
Which inversion? (Answer: _____)

Play this cadence with the given fingering.

Circle the notes in each hand that form a D major triad.

Clap or tap the rhythmic pattern.

3 | THIRD DAY _____ (date)

Play these notes.
Which triad do they form? (Answer: _____)
Which inversion? (Answer: _____)

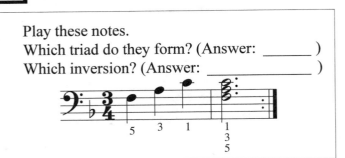

Play this cadence with the given fingering.

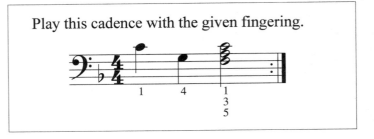

How many solid (blocked) F major triads are there in the LH? (Answer: _____) Circle them.

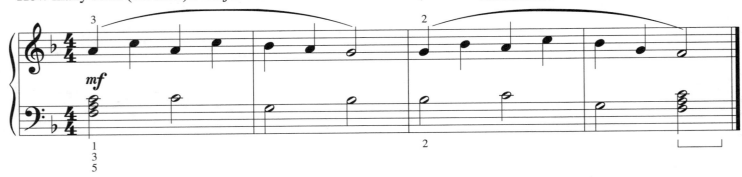

Clap or tap the rhythmic pattern while counting the beats.

4 | FOURTH DAY _____ (date)

Play these notes.
Which triad do they form? (Answer: _____)
Which inversion? (Answer: _____)

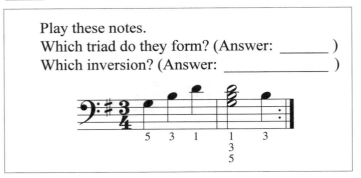

Play this cadence with given fingering.

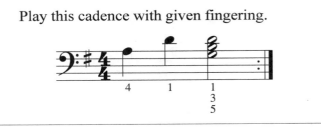

Circle the notes in the RH which form the G major triad in root position.

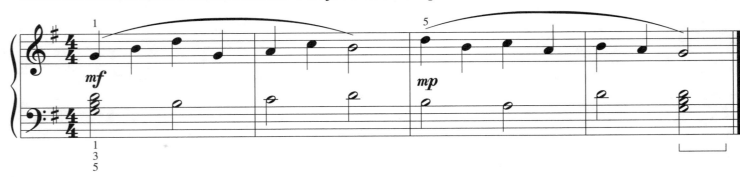

Clap or tap the rhythmic pattern.

Play with the given fingering.

Play with the given fingering.

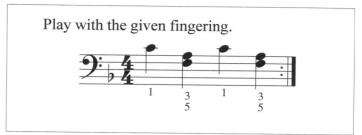

Circle all the repeated notes.

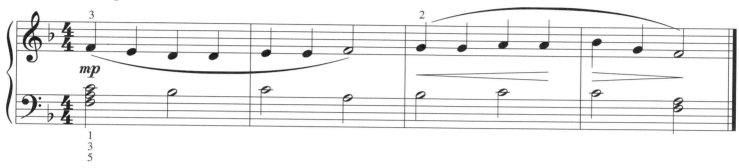

Clap or tap the rhythmic pattern while counting the beats.

DAILY EAR-TRAINING EXERCISES NO. 1

Directions to the student: Complete these ear-training exercises at home.

RHYTHM

Sing, clap, or tap the rhythm of these short melodies: (a) by looking at the music and (b) from memory.

INTERVALS

Play, then sing or hum the two notes of each interval. Identify the interval and write its name underneath.

MELODY PLAYBACK

Name the key of each of the following melodies. For each example, play the tonic chord ONCE. Play the melody TWICE, observing the DIRECTIONS of the notes and the PATTERNS they form. Then play the melody from memory.

DAILY SIGHT-READING EXERCISES No. 2

Directions to the student: Complete one set of sight-reading exercises at each practice session.

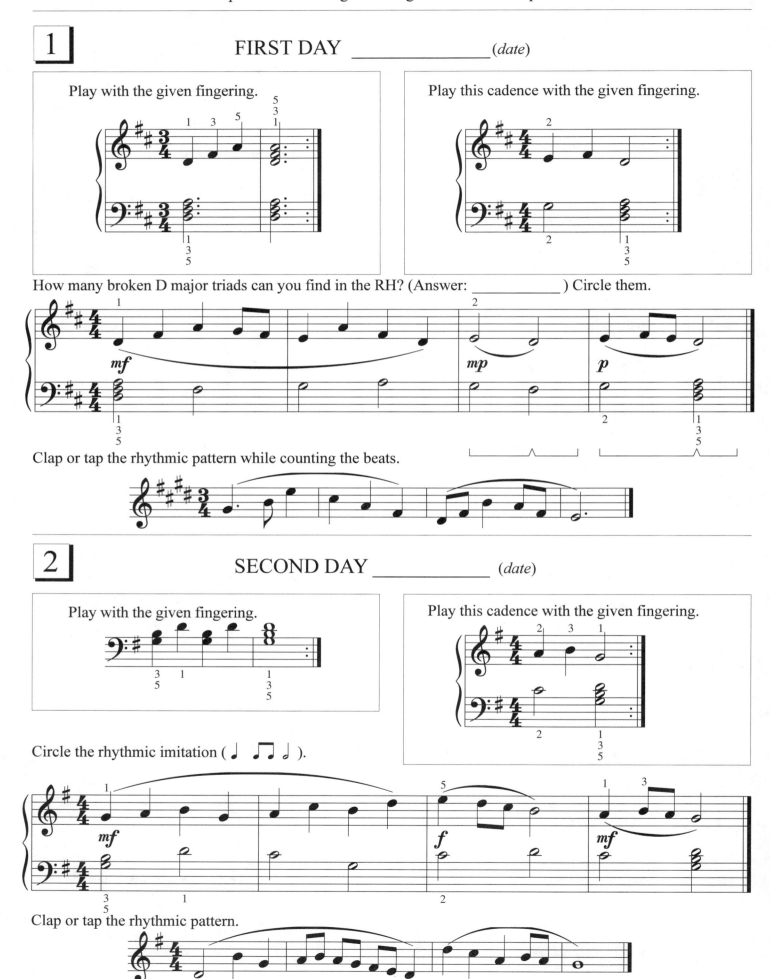

FIRST DAY _____ (date)

Play with the given fingering.

Play this cadence with the given fingering.

How many broken D major triads can you find in the RH? (Answer: _____) Circle them.

Clap or tap the rhythmic pattern while counting the beats.

SECOND DAY _____ (date)

Play with the given fingering.

Play this cadence with the given fingering.

Circle the rhythmic imitation.

Clap or tap the rhythmic pattern.

Play with the given fingering.

Play this cadence with the given fingering.

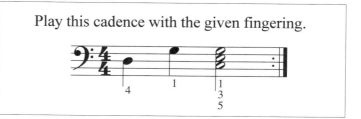

Name the scale formed by the first five notes in the RH. (Answer: _____)

Clap or tap the rhythmic pattern while counting the beats.

FOURTH DAY _____ (*date*)

Play these notes.
Which triad do they form? (Answer: _____)
Which inversion? (Answer: _____)

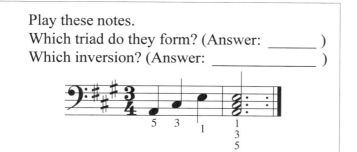

Play this cadence with the given fingering.

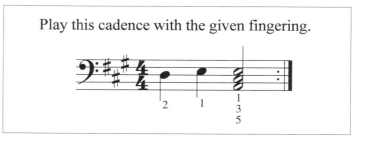

Name the first and last solid (blocked) triads in the LH. (Answer: _____)

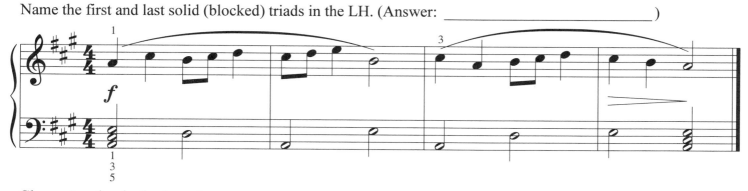

Clap or tap the rhythmic pattern.

5 FIFTH DAY _____ (date)

Play with the given fingering.

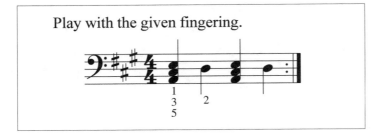

Play this cadence with the given fingering.

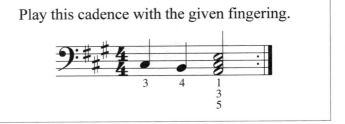

Circle all the intervals of a 3rd and 4th.

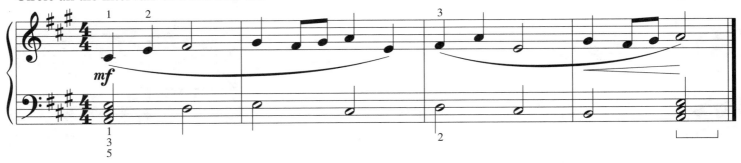

Clap or tap the rhythmic pattern while counting the beats.

DAILY EAR-TRAINING EXERCISES NO. 2

Directions to the student: Complete these ear-training exercises at home.

RHYTHM

Sing, clap, or tap the rhythm of these short melodies: (a) by looking at the music and (b) from memory.

INTERVALS

Play, then sing or hum the two notes of each interval. Identify the interval and write its name underneath.

MELODY PLAYBACK

Name the key of each of the following melodies. For each example, play the tonic chord ONCE. Play the melody TWICE, observing the DIRECTIONS of the notes and the PATTERNS they form. Then play the melody from memory.

Daily Sight-Reading Exercises No. 3

Directions to the student: Complete one set of sight-reading exercises at each practice session.

1   FIRST DAY _____ (*date*)

Play with the given fingering.

Play with the given fingering.

Play, counting the beats.

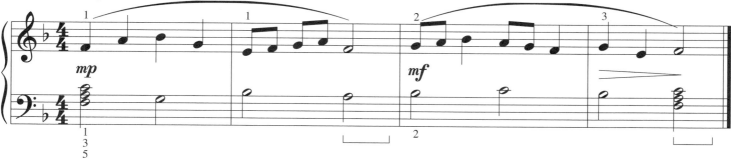

Clap or tap the rhythmic pattern while counting the beats.

2   SECOND DAY _____ (*date*)

Play with the given fingering.

Play with the given fingering.

Name the LH notes as you play.

Clap or tap the rhythmic pattern.

3 | THIRD DAY _____ (date)

Play with the given fingering.

Play with the given fingering.

Play, naming the RH notes.

Clap or tap the rhythmic pattern while counting the beats.

4 | FOURTH DAY _____ (date)

Play with the given fingering.

Play with the given fingering.

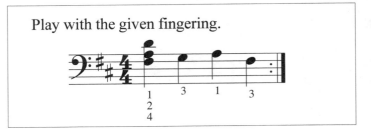

In how many measures do the hands move in contrary motion? (Answer: _____)

Clap or tap the rhythmic pattern.

FIFTH DAY _____ (*date*)

Play with the given fingering.	Play this cadence with the given fingering.
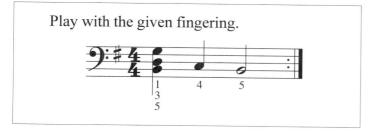	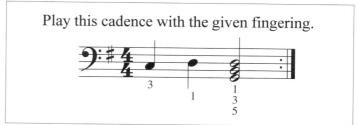

How many different positions of the G major solid (blocked) triad are there in the LH? (Answer: _____)
Name them. (Answer: _____)

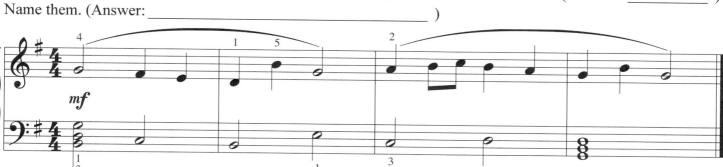

Clap or tap the rhythmic pattern while counting the beats.

DAILY EAR-TRAINING EXERCISES No. 3

Directions to the student: Complete these ear-training exercises at home.

RHYTHM

Sing, clap, or tap the rhythm of these short melodies: (a) by looking at the music and (b) from memory.

INTERVALS

Play, then sing or hum the two notes of each interval. Identify the interval and write its name underneath.

_____ _____   _____ _____

MELODY PLAYBACK

Name the key of each of the following melodies. For each example, play the tonic chord ONCE. Play the melody TWICE, observing the DIRECTIONS of the notes and the PATTERNS they form. Then play the melody from memory.

DAILY SIGHT-READING EXERCISES No. 4

Directions to the student: Complete one set of sight-reading exercises at each practice session.

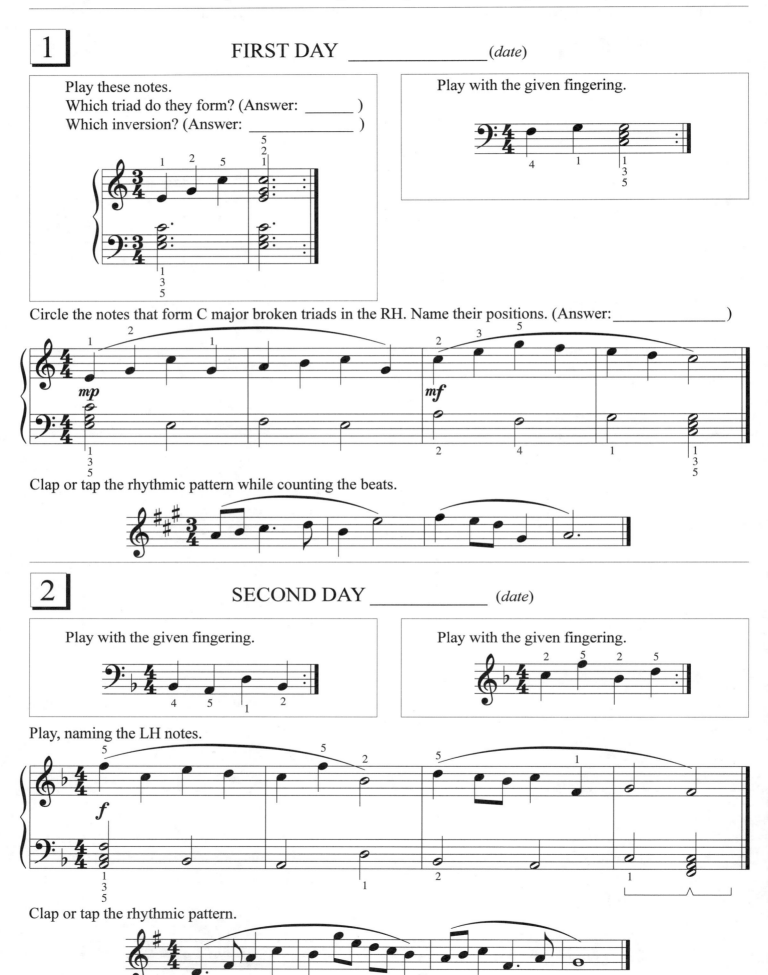

1   FIRST DAY _____ (date)

Play these notes.
Which triad do they form? (Answer: _____)
Which inversion? (Answer: _____)

Play with the given fingering.

Circle the notes that form C major broken triads in the RH. Name their positions. (Answer: _____)

Clap or tap the rhythmic pattern while counting the beats.

2   SECOND DAY _____ (date)

Play with the given fingering.

Play with the given fingering.

Play, naming the LH notes.

Clap or tap the rhythmic pattern.

Play with the given fingering.

Play with the given fingering.

Circle all the intervals of a 4th and 5th.

Clap or tap the rhythmic pattern while counting the beats.

FOURTH DAY _____ (*date*)

Play with the given fingering.

Play with the given fingering.

Play, counting the beats.

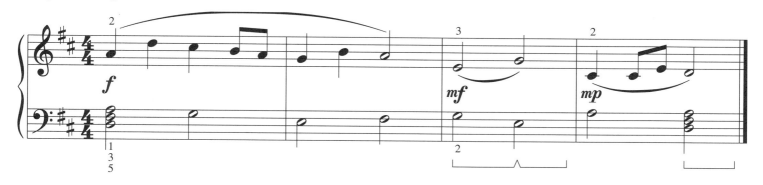

Clap or tap the rhythmic pattern.

5   FIFTH DAY _____ (date)

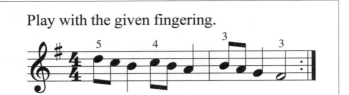

Bracket (⌐) each of the three-note patterns forming the sequence in the RH (♪♪♩).

Clap or tap the rhythmic pattern while counting the beats.

DAILY EAR-TRAINING EXERCISES NO. 4

Directions to the student: Complete these ear-training exercises at home.

RHYTHM

Sing, clap, or tap the rhythm of these short melodies: (a) by looking at the music and (b) from memory.

INTERVALS

Play, then sing or hum the two notes of each interval. Identify the interval and write its name underneath.

_____ _____   _____ _____

MELODY PLAYBACK

Name the key of each of the following melodies. For each example, play the tonic chord ONCE. Play the melody TWICE, observing the DIRECTIONS of the notes and the PATTERNS they form. Then play the melody from memory.

DAILY SIGHT-READING EXERCISES No. 5

Directions to the student: Complete one set of sight-reading exercises at each practice session.

1 FIRST DAY _____ (date)

Play with the given fingering.

Play with the given fingering.

The RH moves to a lower hand position. Name the first note of the new position. (Answer: _____)

Clap or tap the rhythmic pattern while counting the beats.

2 SECOND DAY _____ (date)

Play with the given fingering.

Play with the given fingering.

How many different intervals are there in this piece? Name them. (Answer: _____)

Clap or tap the rhythmic pattern.

20

3   THIRD DAY _____ *(date)*

Play with the given fingering.

Play with the given fingering.

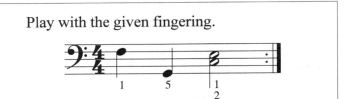

Circle the tied notes in the LH.

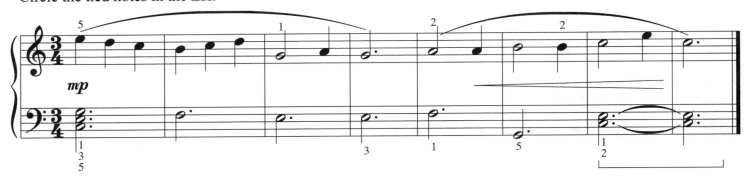

Clap or tap the rhythmic pattern while counting the beats.

---

4   FOURTH DAY _____ *(date)*

Play with the given fingering.

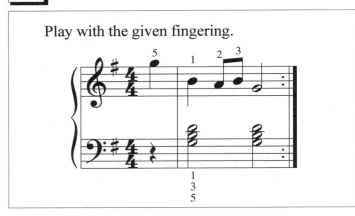

Play with the given fingering.

There are two broken G major triads in the RH. Circle them.

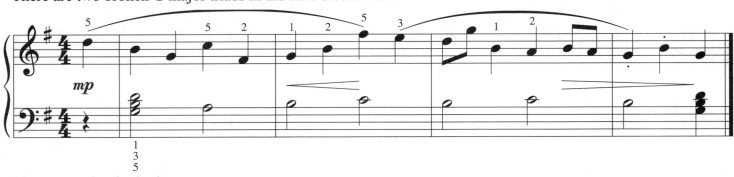

Clap or tap the rhythmic pattern.

5 | FIFTH DAY _____ (date)

Play with the given fingering.

Play with the given fingering.

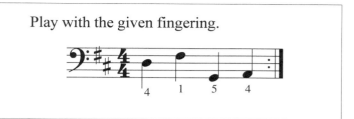

How many different positions of the D major solid (blocked) triad are there in the LH? (Answer: _____)
Name them. (Answer: _____)

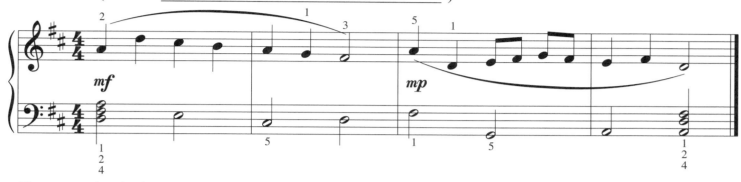

Clap or tap the rhythmic pattern while counting the beats.

DAILY EAR-TRAINING EXERCISES NO. 5

Directions to the student: Complete these ear-training exercises at home.

RHYTHM

Sing, clap, or tap the rhythm of these short melodies: (a) by looking at the music and (b) from memory.

INTERVALS

Play, then sing or hum the two notes of each interval. Identify the interval and write its name underneath.

MELODY PLAYBACK

Name the key of each of the following melodies. For each example, play the tonic chord ONCE. Play the melody TWICE, observing the DIRECTIONS of the notes and the PATTERNS they form. Then play the melody from memory.

DAILY SIGHT-READING EXERCISES NO. 6

Directions to the student: Complete one set of sight-reading exercises at each practice session.

1 FIRST DAY _____ (*date*)

Play with the given fingering.

Play with the given fingering.

Circle all the staccato notes.

Clap or tap the rhythmic pattern while counting the beats.

2 SECOND DAY _____ (*date*)

Play with the given fingering.

Play this cadence with the given fingering.

Play, counting the beats.

Clap or tap the rhythmic pattern.

3 THIRD DAY _____ (*date*)

Play with the given fingering.

Play this cadence with the given fingering.

Name the two notes that form the upbeat in the RH. (Answer: _____)

Clap or tap the rhythmic pattern while counting the beats.

4 FOURTH DAY _____ (*date*)

Play with the given fingering.

Play this cadence with the given fingering.

Circle the notes that form the last five notes of this melodic scale. Name the key. (Answer:_____)

Clap or tap the rhythmic pattern.

Play with the given fingering.

Play with the given fingering.

Bracket the two measures in the RH that have rhythmic imitation.

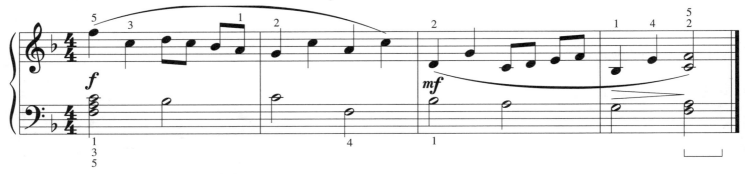

Clap or tap the rhythmic pattern while counting the beats.

DAILY EAR-TRAINING EXERCISES No. 6

Directions to the student: Complete these ear-training exercises at home.

RHYTHM

Sing, clap, or tap the rhythm of these short melodies: (a) by looking at the music and (b) from memory.

INTERVALS

Play, then sing or hum the two notes of each interval. Identify the interval and write its name underneath.

MELODY PLAYBACK

Name the key of each of the following melodies. For each example, play the tonic chord ONCE. Play the melody TWICE, observing the DIRECTIONS of the notes and the PATTERNS they form. Then play the melody from memory.

DAILY SIGHT-READING EXERCISES NO. 7

Directions to the student: Complete one set of sight-reading exercises at each practice session.

1 FIRST DAY _____ (*date*)

Play with the given fingering.

Play with the given fingering.

Bracket the RH notes which form the melodic repetition.

J.-B. Duvernoy

Clap or tap the rhythmic pattern while counting the beats.

2 SECOND DAY _____ (*date*)

Play with the given fingering.

Play with the given fingering.

Circle the repeated notes.

Clap or tap the rhythmic pattern.

26

3 THIRD DAY _____ (date)

Play with the given fingering.

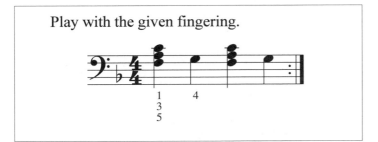

Play with the given fingering.

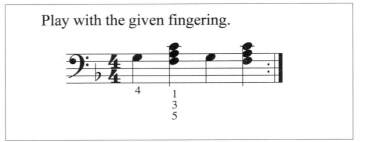

Circle all the melodic intervals of a 3rd and 4th.

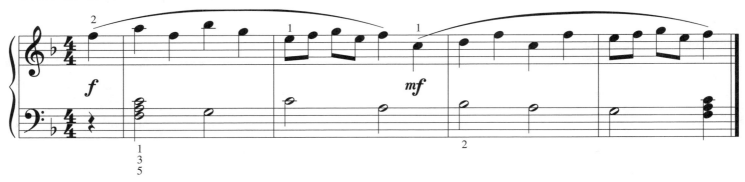

Clap or tap the rhythmic pattern while counting the beats.

4 FOURTH DAY _____ (date)

Play with the given fingering.

Play with the given articulation.

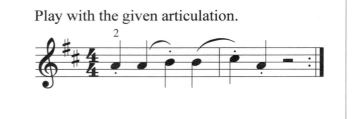

Circle all the staccato notes.

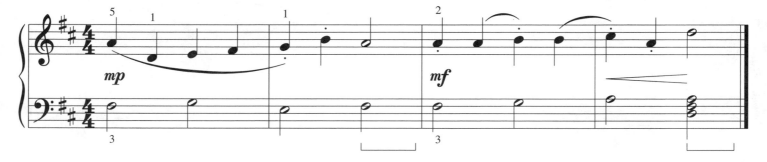

Clap or tap the rhythmic pattern.

Play with the given fingering.

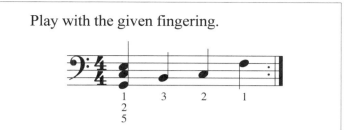

Play this cadence with the given fingering.

Play, counting the beats.

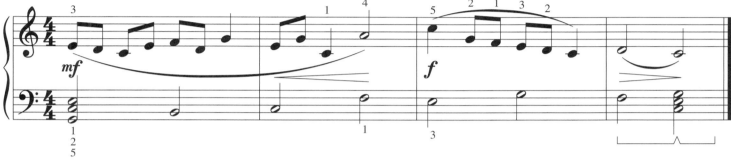

Clap or tap the rhythmic pattern while counting the beats.

DAILY EAR-TRAINING EXERCISES NO. 7

Directions to the student: Complete these ear-training exercises at home.

RHYTHM

Sing, clap, or tap the rhythm of these short melodies: (a) by looking at the music and (b) from memory.

INTERVALS

Play, then sing or hum the two notes of each interval. Identify the interval and write its name underneath.

MELODY PLAYBACK

Name the key of each of the following melodies. For each example, play the tonic chord ONCE. Play the melody TWICE, observing the DIRECTIONS of the notes and the PATTERNS they form. Then play the melody from memory.

DAILY SIGHT-READING EXERCISES No. 8

Directions to the student: Complete one set of sight-reading exercises at each practice session.

1 FIRST DAY _____ (*date*)

Play with the given fingering.

Play with the given fingering.

Name the highest and lowest notes in this piece. (Answer: _____)

Clap or tap the rhythmic pattern while counting the beats.

2 SECOND DAY _____ (*date*)

Play with the given fingering.

Play this cadence with the given fingering.

How many different positions of the F major solid (blocked) triad are there in the LH? (Answer: _____)
Name them. (Answer: _____)

Clap or tap the rhythmic pattern.

3   THIRD DAY _____ (*date*)

Play with the given fingering.

Play with the given fingering.

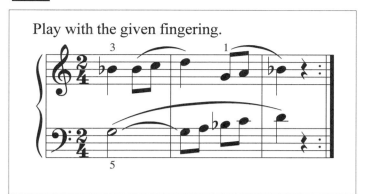

Play, counting the beats.

F. Wohlfahrt

Clap or tap the rhythmic pattern while counting the beats.

4   FOURTH DAY _____ (*date*)

Play with the given fingering.

Play this cadence with the given fingering.

How many times do you hear the rhythmic motif (♫ ♩ ♩)? (Answer: _____)

Clap or tap the rhythmic pattern.

5 FIFTH DAY _____ (*date*)

Play with the given fingering.

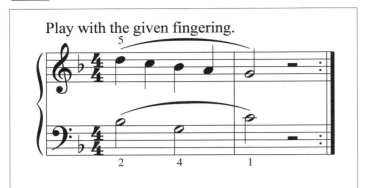

Play with the given fingering.

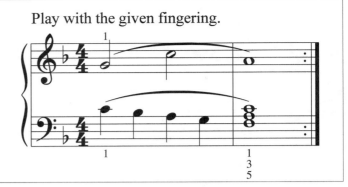

How many broken and solid (blocked) triads are there in this piece? (Answer: _____)

Clap or tap the rhythmic pattern while counting the beats.

DAILY EAR-TRAINING EXERCISES No. 8

Directions to the student: Complete these ear-training exercises at home.

RHYTHM

Sing, clap, or tap the rhythm of these short melodies: (a) by looking at the music and (b) from memory.

INTERVALS

Play, then sing or hum the two notes of each interval. Identify the interval and write its name underneath.

MELODY PLAYBACK

Name the key of each of each of the following melodies. For each example, play the tonic chord ONCE. Play the melody TWICE, observing the DIRECTIONS of the notes and the PATTERNS they form. Then play the melody from memory.

DAILY SIGHT-READING EXERCISES No. 9

Directions to the student: Complete one set of sight-reading exercises at each practice session.

1 FIRST DAY _____ (date)

Play with the given fingering.

Play with the given fingering.

Name the LH notes as you play.

J.L. Krebs

Clap or tap the rhythmic pattern while counting the beats.

2 SECOND DAY _____ (date)

Play with the given fingering.

Play this cadence with the given fingering.

Play, counting the beats.

Clap or tap the rhythmic pattern.

3   THIRD DAY _____ (*date*)

Play with the given fingering.

Play this cadence with the given fingering.

The LH moves to a lower hand position. Name the first note of the new position. (Answer: _____)

Clap or tap the rhythmic pattern while counting the beats.

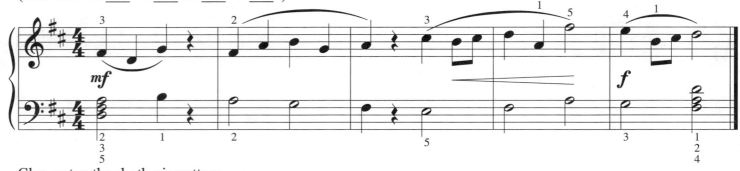

4   FOURTH DAY _____ (*date*)

Play with the given fingering.

Play this cadence with the given fingering.

How many notes are there in each of the four RH phrases?
(Answer: 1. ___   2. ___   3. ___   4. ___)

Clap or tap the rhythmic pattern.

5 FIFTH DAY _____ (*date*)

Play with the given fingering.

Play this cadence with the given fingering.

On which beat do the RH rests fall? (Answer: _____) Circle them.

Clap or tap the rhythmic pattern while counting the beats.

DAILY EAR-TRAINING EXERCISES NO. 9

Directions to the student: Complete these ear-training exercises at home.

RHYTHM

Sing, clap, or tap the rhythm of these short melodies: (a) by looking at the music and (b) from memory.

INTERVALS

Play, then sing or hum the two notes of each interval. Identify the interval and write its name underneath.

MELODY PLAYBACK

Name the key of each of the following melodies. For each example, play the tonic chord ONCE. Play the melody TWICE, observing the DIRECTIONS of the notes and the PATTERNS they form. Then play the melody from memory.

DAILY SIGHT-READING EXERCISES No. 10

Directions to the student: Complete one set of sight-reading exercises at each practice session.

1   FIRST DAY _____ (*date*)

Play with the given fingering.

Play with the given fingering.

Bracket the D major scale from dominant to dominant.

Clap or tap the rhythmic pattern while counting the beats.

2   SECOND DAY _____ (*date*)

Play with the given fingering.

Play this cadence with the given fingering.

How many times is the following rhythmic pattern used (♩ | ♩ ♫ ♩)? (Answer: _____) Bracket them.

Clap or tap the rhythmic pattern.

3 **THIRD DAY** _____ (*date*)

Play with the given fingering.

Play with the given fingering.

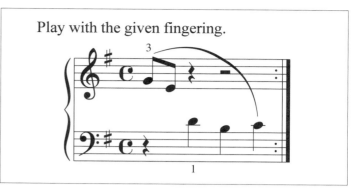

Bracket the G major scale.

E. Breslaur

Clap or tap the rhythmic pattern while counting the beats.

4 **FOURTH DAY** _____ (*date*)

Play with the given fingering.

Play this cadence with the given fingering.

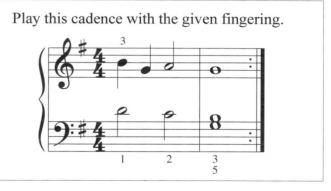

Play, naming the LH notes.

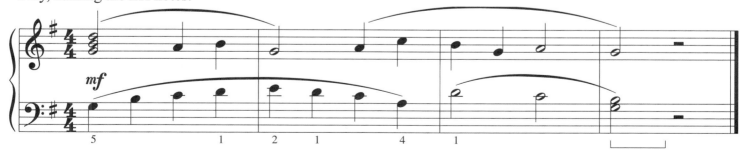

Clap or tap the rhythmic pattern.

5 | FIFTH DAY _____ (date)

Play with the given fingering.

Play this cadence with the given fingering.

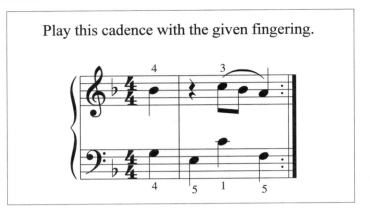

Name the two notes that are found in every measure of the LH. (Answer: _____) Circle them.

Clap or tap the rhythmic pattern while counting the beats.

DAILY EAR-TRAINING EXERCISES No. 10

Directions to the student: Complete these ear-training exercises at home.

RHYTHM

Sing, clap, or tap the rhythm of these short melodies: (a) by looking at the music and (b) from memory.

INTERVALS

Play, then sing or hum the two notes of each interval. Identify the interval and write its name underneath.

MELODY PLAYBACK

Name the key of each of the following melodies. For each example, play the tonic chord ONCE. Play the melody TWICE, observing the DIRECTIONS of the notes and the PATTERNS they form. Then play the melody from memory.

★ Four Star Test No. 1 ★

GIVEN BY THE TEACHER AT THE LESSON

SIGHT-READING TEST

Teacher's grading

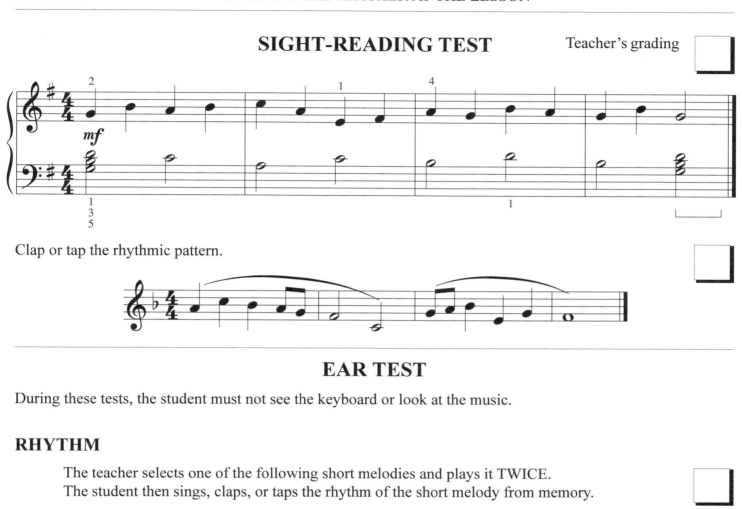

Clap or tap the rhythmic pattern.

EAR TEST

During these tests, the student must not see the keyboard or look at the music.

RHYTHM

The teacher selects one of the following short melodies and plays it TWICE.
The student then sings, claps, or taps the rhythm of the short melody from memory.

INTERVALS

The teacher selects and names each of the following intervals and plays the first note ONCE.
The student then sings or hums the other note; OR
The teacher plays an interval in broken form ONCE and the student *identifies* (names) it by ear.
The teacher then repeats this procedure with several other intervals.

MELODY PLAYBACK

The teacher selects one of the following melodies, names the key, plays the tonic chord ONCE,
and then plays the melody TWICE. The student then plays back the melody from memory.

For additional material, see the series *Melody Playback/Singback* and *Rhythm Clapback/Singback*.

★ Four Star Test No. 2 ★

Given by the Teacher at the Lesson

SIGHT-READING TEST   Teacher's grading

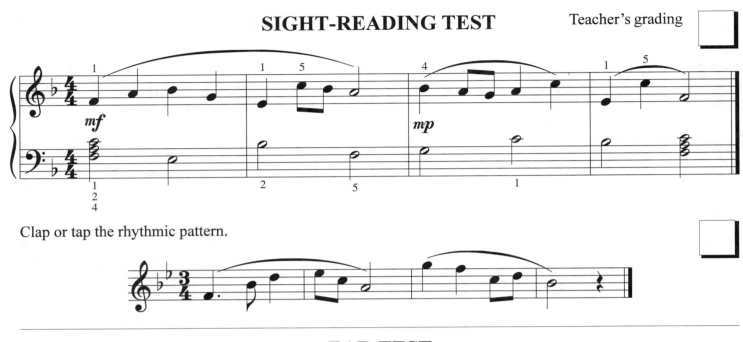

Clap or tap the rhythmic pattern.

EAR TEST

During these tests, the student must not see the keyboard or look at the music.

RHYTHM

The teacher selects one of the following short melodies and plays it TWICE.
The student then sings, claps, or taps the rhythm of the short melody from memory.

INTERVALS

The teacher selects and names each of the following intervals and plays the first note ONCE.
The student then sings or hums the other note; OR
The teacher plays an interval in broken form ONCE and the student *identifies* (names) it by ear.
The teacher then repeats this procedure with several other intervals.

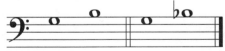

MELODY PLAYBACK

The teacher selects one of the following melodies, names the key, plays the tonic chord ONCE,
and then plays the melody TWICE. The student then plays back the melody from memory.

For additional material, see the series *Melody Playback/Singback* and *Rhythm Clapback/Singback*.

★ FOUR STAR TEST No. 3 ★

GIVEN BY THE TEACHER AT THE LESSON

SIGHT-READING TEST

Teacher's grading

Clap or tap the rhythmic pattern.

EAR TEST

During these tests, the student must not see the keyboard or look at the music.

RHYTHM

The teacher selects one of the following short melodies and plays it TWICE.
The student then sings, claps, or taps the rhythm of the short melody from memory.

INTERVALS

The teacher selects and names each of the following intervals and plays the first note ONCE.
The student then sings or hums the other note; OR
The teacher plays an interval in broken form ONCE and the student *identifies* (names) it by ear.
The teacher then repeats this procedure with several other intervals.

 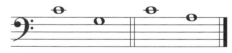

MELODY PLAYBACK

The teacher selects one of the following melodies, names the key, plays the tonic chord ONCE,
and then plays the melody TWICE. The student then plays back the melody from memory.

For additional material, see the series *Melody Playback/Singback* and *Rhythm Clapback/Singback*.

★ FOUR STAR TEST NO. 4 ★

GIVEN BY THE TEACHER AT THE LESSON

SIGHT-READING TEST

Teacher's grading

Clap or tap the rhythmic pattern.

EAR TEST

During these tests, the student must not see the keyboard or look at the music.

RHYTHM

The teacher selects one of the following short melodies and plays it TWICE.
The student then sings, claps, or taps the rhythm of the short melody from memory.

INTERVALS

The teacher selects and names each of the following intervals and plays the first note ONCE.
The student then sings or hums the other note; OR
The teacher plays an interval in broken form ONCE and the student *identifies* (names) it by ear.
The teacher then repeats this procedure with several other intervals.

MELODY PLAYBACK

The teacher selects one of the following melodies, names the key, plays the tonic chord ONCE,
and then plays the melody TWICE. The student then plays back the melody from memory.

For additional material, see the series *Melody Playback/Singback* and *Rhythm Clapback/Singback*.

★ FOUR STAR TEST NO. 5 ★

GIVEN BY THE TEACHER AT THE LESSON

SIGHT-READING TEST

Teacher's grading

Clap or tap the rhythmic pattern.

EAR TEST

During these tests, the student must not see the keyboard or look at the music.

RHYTHM

The teacher selects one of the following short melodies and plays it TWICE.
The student then sings, claps, or taps the rhythm of the short melody from memory.

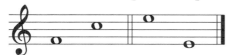 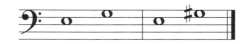

INTERVALS

The teacher selects and names each of the following intervals and plays the first note ONCE.
The student then sings or hums the other note; OR
The teacher plays an interval in broken form ONCE and the student *identifies* (names) it by ear.
The teacher then repeats this procedure with several other intervals.

MELODY PLAYBACK

The teacher selects one of the following melodies, names the key, plays the tonic chord ONCE,
and then plays the melody TWICE. The student then plays back the melody from memory.

For additional material, see the series *Melody Playback/Singback* and *Rhythm Clapback/Singback*.

★ FOUR STAR TEST NO. 6 ★

GIVEN BY THE TEACHER AT THE LESSON

SIGHT-READING TEST

Teacher's grading

Clap or tap the rhythmic pattern.

EAR TEST

During these tests, the student must not see the keyboard or look at the music.

RHYTHM

The teacher selects one of the following short melodies and plays it TWICE.
The student then sings, claps, or taps the rhythm of the short melody from memory.

INTERVALS

The teacher selects and names each of the following intervals and plays the first note ONCE.
The student then sings or hums the other note; OR
The teacher plays an interval in broken form ONCE and the student *identifies* (names) it by ear.
The teacher then repeats this procedure with several other intervals.

MELODY PLAYBACK

The teacher selects one of the following melodies, names the key, plays the tonic chord ONCE,
and then plays the melody TWICE. The student then plays back the melody from memory.

For additional material, see the series *Melody Playback/Singback* and *Rhythm Clapback/Singback*.

★ FOUR STAR TEST No. 7 ★

GIVEN BY THE TEACHER AT THE LESSON

SIGHT-READING TEST

Teacher's grading

Clap or tap the rhythmic pattern.

EAR TEST

During these tests, the student must not see the keyboard or look at the music.

RHYTHM

The teacher selects one of the following short melodies and plays it TWICE.
The student then sings, claps, or taps the rhythm of the short melody from memory.

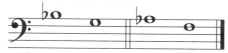

INTERVALS

The teacher selects and names each of the following intervals and plays the first note ONCE.
The student then sings or hums the other note; OR
The teacher plays an interval in broken form ONCE and the student *identifies* (names) it by ear.
The teacher then repeats this procedure with several other intervals.

MELODY PLAYBACK

The teacher selects one of the following melodies, names the key, plays the tonic chord ONCE,
and then plays the melody TWICE. The student then plays back the melody from memory.

For additional material, see the series *Melody Playback/Singback* and *Rhythm Clapback/Singback*.

★ Four Star Test No. 8 ★

GIVEN BY THE TEACHER AT THE LESSON

SIGHT-READING TEST

Teacher's grading

Clap or tap the rhythmic pattern.

EAR TEST

During these tests, the student must not see the keyboard or look at the music.

RHYTHM

The teacher selects one of the following short melodies and plays it TWICE.
The student then sings, claps, or taps the rhythm of the short melody from memory.

INTERVALS

The teacher selects and names each of the following intervals and plays the first note ONCE.
The student then sings or hums the other note; OR
The teacher plays an interval in broken form ONCE and the student *identifies* (names) it by ear.
The teacher then repeats this procedure with several other intervals.

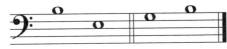

MELODY PLAYBACK

The teacher selects one of the following melodies, names the key, plays the tonic chord ONCE,
and then plays the melody TWICE. The student then plays back the melody from memory.

For additional material, see the series *Melody Playback/Singback* and *Rhythm Clapback/Singback*.

★ FOUR STAR TEST NO. 9 ★

GIVEN BY THE TEACHER AT THE LESSON

SIGHT-READING TEST

Teacher's grading

Con grazia

E. Breslaur

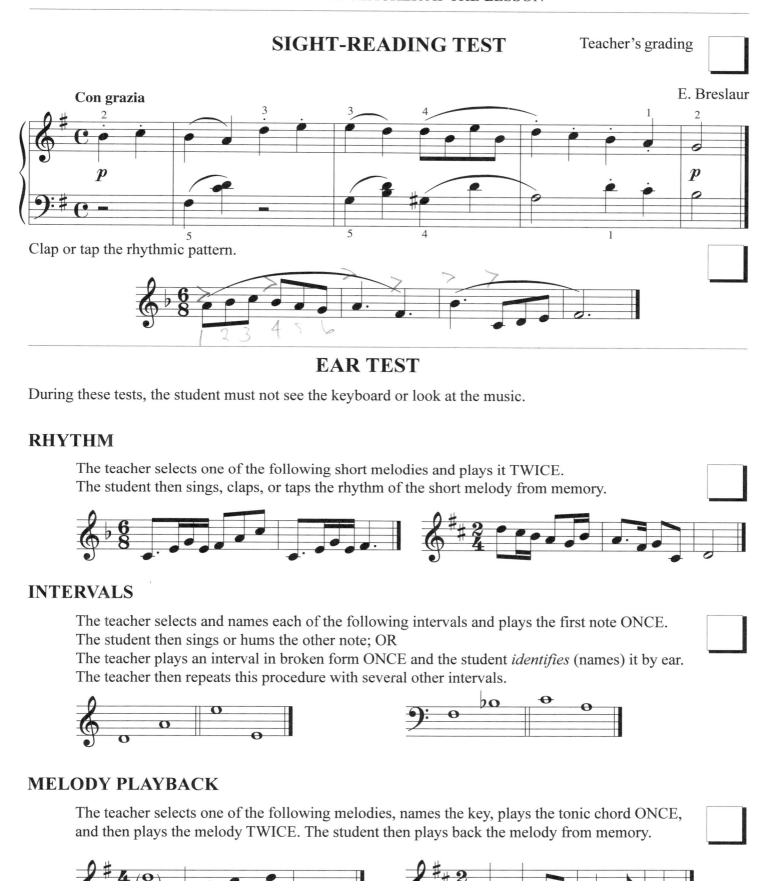

Clap or tap the rhythmic pattern.

EAR TEST

During these tests, the student must not see the keyboard or look at the music.

RHYTHM

The teacher selects one of the following short melodies and plays it TWICE.
The student then sings, claps, or taps the rhythm of the short melody from memory.

INTERVALS

The teacher selects and names each of the following intervals and plays the first note ONCE.
The student then sings or hums the other note; OR
The teacher plays an interval in broken form ONCE and the student *identifies* (names) it by ear.
The teacher then repeats this procedure with several other intervals.

MELODY PLAYBACK

The teacher selects one of the following melodies, names the key, plays the tonic chord ONCE,
and then plays the melody TWICE. The student then plays back the melody from memory.

For additional material, see the series *Melody Playback/Singback* and *Rhythm Clapback/Singback*.

★ FOUR STAR TEST No. 10 ★

GIVEN BY THE TEACHER AT THE LESSON

SIGHT-READING TEST

Teacher's grading

Clap or tap the rhythmic pattern.

EAR TEST

During these tests, the student must not see the keyboard or look at the music.

RHYTHM

The teacher selects one of the following short melodies and plays it TWICE.
The student then sings, claps, or taps the rhythm of the short melody from memory.

INTERVALS

The teacher selects and names each of the following intervals and plays the first note ONCE.
The student then sings or hums the other note; OR
The teacher plays an interval in broken form ONCE and the student *identifies* (names) it by ear.
The teacher then repeats this procedure with several other intervals.

MELODY PLAYBACK

The teacher selects one of the following melodies, names the key, plays the tonic chord ONCE,
and then plays the melody TWICE. The student then plays back the melody from memory.

For additional material, see the series *Melody Playback/Singback* and *Rhythm Clapback/Singback*.

★ FINAL FOUR STAR TEST ★

This test will be given before filling in and signing the Certificate of Achievement.

SIGHT-READING TEST

Teacher's grading

Clap or tap the rhythmic pattern.

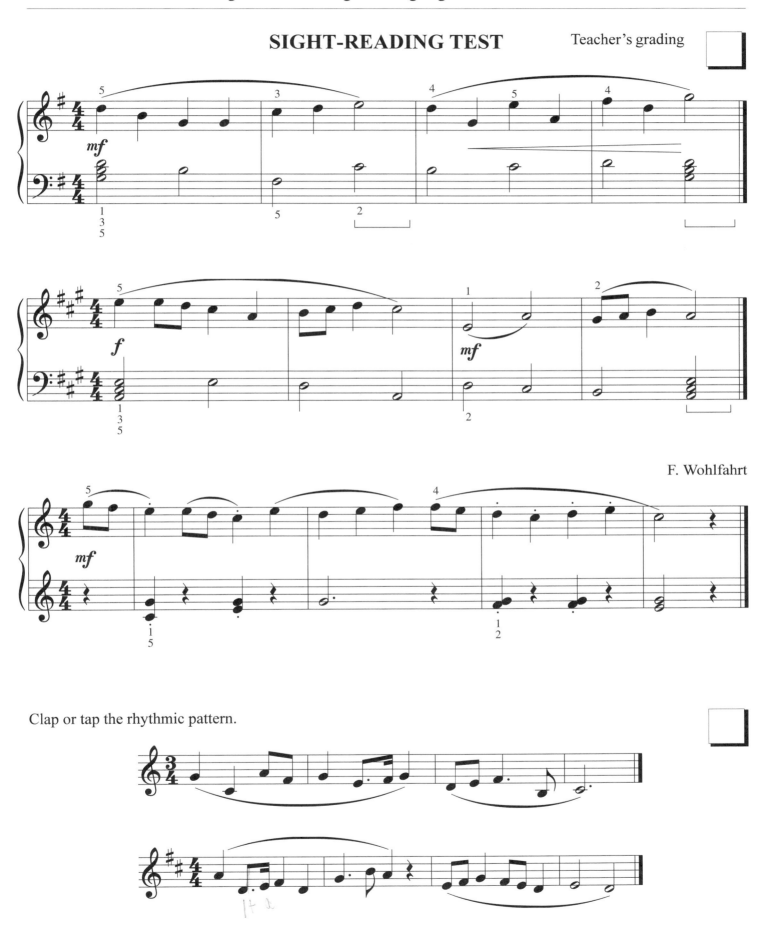

F. Wohlfahrt

EAR TEST

During these tests, the student must not see the keyboard or look at the music.

RHYTHM

The teacher selects one of the following short melodies and plays it TWICE.
The student then sings, claps, or taps the rhythm of the short melody from memory.

INTERVALS

The teacher selects and names each of the following intervals and plays the first note ONCE.
The student then sings or hums the other note; OR
The teacher plays an interval in broken form ONCE and the student *identifies* (names) it by ear.
The teacher then repeats this procedure with several other intervals.

MELODY PLAYBACK

The teacher selects one of the following melodies, names the key, plays the tonic chord ONCE,
and then plays the melody TWICE. The student then plays back the melody from memory.

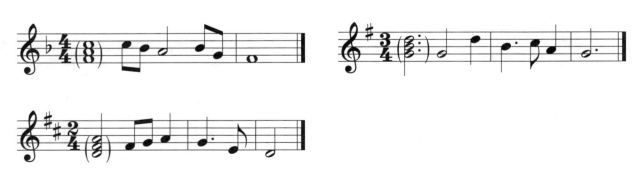

For additional material, see the series *Melody Playback/Singback* and *Rhythm Clapback/Singback*.

ADDITIONAL PIECES IN PREPARATION FOR LEVEL 5

Students should play the following examples with their teacher at the lesson, or as assigned for home practice.

M. Clementi

12) **Allegretto semplice**

A. Brunner

16)

17)

18)

Allegretto scherzando

F. Wohlfahrt

C. Gurlitt

A.E. Müller

A.E. Müller